Village Fox

Richard Cave

Stairwell Books //

Published by Stairwell Books
161 Lowther Street
York, YO31 7LZ

www.stairwellbooks.co.uk
@stairwellbooks

Village Fox © 2025 Richard Cave and Stairwell Books

All rights reserved. No part of this publication may be reproduced, stored in or introduced into a retrieval system, or transmitted, in any form, or by any means (electronic, mechanical, photocopying, recording, e-book or otherwise) without the prior written permission of the author.

The moral rights of the author have been asserted.

Cover image: Dawn Treacher

Paperback ISBN: 978-1-917334-08-2

Table of Contents

Inside this old skin	1
Still Asking Why ...	2
Looking Back ...	3
The Election Canvasser	4
Rationing ended the year Mary was born	5
An Unlost Memory	8
The Making of Us	10
We didn't have a name for them in our house	11
Growing out of it?	12
Old man and son	14
No Words	15
Remembering Uncle Ray	16
Bumping into Baz	17
Hottest Summer since '76	18
Train ride to Paddington	20
Hometown Visit	22
Sixpence	23
Those Eyes	25
I never expected ...	27
Firework	28
L.O.V.E.	29
Following Too Much Cheese	30
Fingerprints On My Mind	31
Jessica	32
I missed you today	34
I knew the day we met	35
When the dogs have left	36
Village Fox	37
The Passing of 1000 Gulls	38
I Picked up the Present	39
The Silence of Yesterday	41
Last time we met	42
The Real You	44

I passed a group of moist-eyed men	45
A Crack Appeared	46
The Valley of the Shadow	47
Sorry for being so rubbish	48
To A Friend	49
The Visit	50
Haikus	51
What is Truth?	52
An Old Man Told Me	53
Seeking Open Water	55
Dancing beneath the Doodlebugs	56
Colours of our Land	58
Gravestones	59
Where they drowned the Witches	60
Just Walking Home	61
The Kiss	62
LGB with the T	63
White Knight	65
The Fisherman's Cottage	67
Walking the Days Away	68
Girl with the Violin	69
Take These Words	71

Inside this old skin

Within this creased, winter-pale skin
once stood an angry young man.

Beneath this greying head,
stiff-limbed, aching, fueled by various pills,
now stands an older wiser man;

both still raging ⚡

Still Asking Why ...

I came into this world piglet pink
hairless as an egg
thinly disguised as
   ... well ...
someone normal,
don't we all.

I grew up asking Why?
Why do only men have beards?
Why are there twelve numbers on a clock?
If Everest is the highest mountain, why can't I see it?
Why are bubbles round?
Why do dogs sniff bottoms?
Why can't we send a lorry full of food to Africa to feed the
hungry children?

And now, after why, after why, after why,
Why am I still asking Why?
Why do we need Pride?
Why must we say "Black Lives Matter"?
Why is Strange Fruit still hanging from the tree?
Why are keyworkers the lowest paid?
Why are we still buying slave-sewn shirts?
Why can't we give peace a chance?

I guess I'll leave this world
a battle scarred, bristle-backed old boar,
snuffling in my food
still thinly disguised as someone normal

still asking why.

Looking Back ...

When I grow rich
I'll do some good

A humble philanthropist

A jean-clad Robin Hood
slipping unnoticed into lives
leaving a legacy

Maybe a 21st century St Nick
painting smiles onto troubled faces

A benevolent hermit
enigmatic, yet revered

When I visit strange, distant lands
where skinny arms hold
skinnier children with
empty pockets and emptier bellies
I'll freely give of my riches and
photograph their smiling
grateful faces to frame
to hang upon my wall

But, now –
looking round,
I see how rich I have become
And see how little good I've done ⁄⁄

The Election Canvasser

Back in the day
when I used to work;
that is, proper work,
rather than tapping keyboards
and telling others how to work;
back in the day,
there I was,
tools in hand
ready to ascend
the dizzy heights of a suburban semi's gutter.
He appeared,
walking up the garden path
with the look of a man ordered by his wife
to complain in a high-class restaurant,
and,
caught in the glare of fellow diners
has no option but to comply.

He handed me a leaflet:
"Ten reasons why you should vote
for Margaret Thatcher."
Well, I'm not normally ready with a quick riposte;
he would usually be five minutes down the road
by the time a suitable reply reached my lips;
but, on this occasion,

"I can think of more than ten reasons why I shouldn't vote
for Margaret Thatcher."

With the look of a man who's
found the one he's been searching for,
the one who understands,
only to see them board a ferry,
never to return,
and,
gazing from the quayside turns to leave;
"Yes," he said. "Yes, I expect you can." //

Rationing ended the year Mary was born

Rationing ended the year Mary was born
but little changed on Ardknock Row
Mum still served up margarine and spam
Dad spent too much in the Rose & Crown

Mary remembered the day more than her dad
when black-tied uncles patted her shoulders
and hatted, moist-eyed aunties stooped to kiss her cheek
or hand a tube of Parma Violets,
but as the last black limo pulled away,
little had changed on Ardknock Row

The first song Mary remembers was
The Loco-Motion
but it wasn't until *I Want to Hold Your Hand*
it really clicked
She dreamt about jostling the hysterical,
screaming crowds and Paul
reaching down – their outstretched fingers meeting –
eyes locked.
By the time she was old enough, it was too late
Besides she'd got a job,
got into trouble, got the sack, got married
had the baby,
and another,
they moved into No. 12 in time for No. 3
back on Ardknock Row

Then came the strikes, the picket lines, police lines, battle lines,
headlines, deadlines, party lines,
end of the line.
The pits closed
Frankie's closed
Dot's Diner closed

Pugh's Homeware (Estd. 1929) closed
Bevan & Bevan closed
cinemas, hairdressers, B&Bs and car-dealers closed
doors closed
a chapter closed.
White-washed boards went up in High Street windows,
For Sale boards went up outside No. 12,
Then No. 3
and 33,
No.6, No. 9, No.12, No. 22 ...
Mary lost count
Boards hung like desolate prayer flags,
bleak reminders of her worthlessness
until ...... one by one the flags came down
prayers and pleas unanswered:
No one bought or sold
or even dared to hope on Ardknock Row

Slowly,
very slowly,
industry crept back up the valley,
tentative and wary, like urban foxes
drawn in by human debris.
Money returned
Life returned
Salesmen returned
offering stone-cladding and double-glazing
and insurance for things that would never happen.
(Mary plumped for double glazing)
And façades looked brighter on Ardknock Row

And now?
Now, Mary pops round to No. 9 for coffee
and listens to complaints about stone cladding,
(Mary's glad she opted for double glazing)
When they're flush they walk into town for a Costa
or to buy inexpensive gifts for the grandchildren.
Mary never mentions it, but she once saw her son-in-law
queueing for the foodbank, so, ▢

every Friday she takes the bus to Tesco
and drops his favourite cereal and some beans in the
donation box
and, although she's never been heard to swear,
last week she stood and screamed
"How the xxxx have we got foodbanks in 2022!"

Yes, bugger all has changed
for those on Ardknock Row ⁄⁄

An Unlost Memory

I played rugby there once,
years ago.
I don't remember the score
or even the result.
But I do remember the ice,
the mud,
the red raw, coal dust encrusted knees,
every tackle, every fall:
ice, mud, coal dust.

And, I remember the scar:
the scar on the hillside,
the slice of village missing
and the scar on our memories.
We all knew Aberfan for one thing.
The scar dominated our thoughts,
the scar was our thoughts.
None of us knew anything else about Aberfan,
Except:
'Aberfan'.
The name meant disaster.
Not village.
Not mining town.
Just disaster.

I was six years old,
this, the first news to penetrate my child bubble,
a silent sorrow clung like the Towy fog.
Grief oozed from the grown-ups who
gave money they couldn't afford,
money destined for: who knows?
The Sunday roast, my birthday, new shoes?

I grew up with Aberfan,
as I grew up with a sister

I was too young to remember.
Most of the time,
the door is closed,
the memories shut away,
Aberfan and Gwyneth
as remote as Saigon, or Gunga Din

But somedays ...
Somedays ...
They sneak up, dog-breath quiet
stow beneath the duvet,
squat silent on the landing,
a shadow amongst the shadows
Somedays I am the unlost memory
Somedays I am the scarred hillside
The unhealed wound.
Somedays
I am Aberfan. ⁄⁄

The Making of Us

Just because you moved in when I was 12 months old –
that don't make you my sister
and just because pocket money was doled out in equal amounts
and Christmas stockings filled with equal precision,
that don't make you my sister
Just because we called the same two people
"mum" and "dad",
or because you cried more than me at their funerals:
that don't make you my sister.

But it's the love we've shared over fading years,
a love born amongst trawlers and refineries,
watered on fertile dairy plains,
knotted tighter over distant miles.
It's the family we've knitted out of wool shorn from different sheep;
carved from the wood of separate trees;
rocks hewn from neighbouring quarries:
this,
this is what makes you my sister.

We didn't have a name for them in our house

We didn't have a name for them in our house
I didn't know they didn't have a name
I can't remember them being a thing
They must have been there:
Quiet
Ignored

Jane down the road introduced me to the name,
"I've just farted," she said
I didn't know what she was talking about,
I didn't like to ask,
But I had learnt a new word,
I soon learnt its meaning too:
(Jane seemed to fart a lot)
I soon learnt other names for it:
Parp, pump, trump.

But,
We never had a name for them in our house
We'd ignore them –
perhaps they would go away:

Like beggars
the homeless,
extra-marital pregnancies
mental illness

Of course, they never did.

Growing out of it?

I was told I'd grow out of it.

No timescale was given
But,
I think,
less than forty-five years was envisaged.

Generally referred to as "that Infernal Din"
or, less frequently,
"that unearthly racket"
it was maligned with the all-encompassing label:
"Pop" Music.

No point in explaining that Dylan or Jethro Tull,
Judas Priest or Ram Jam weren't "pop".
No point is saying that Aretha Franklin or Marvin Gaye
had soul,
Were soul.

Of course, it wasn't just the music.
It was everything from
the pelvic sway of Elvis
Mark Bolan's make-up
The behavior of Keith Moon
The sexual ambiguity of Bowie
The phallic symbolism of the guitar
But, most of all,
it was the hair.
From the Beatles to Barclay James Harvest,
The Moody Blues to Motorhead,
Big Hair was in.

I tried to grow long hair, but,
due to its consistency, akin to that of an unwashed racoon,
it wouldn't flow down my back, like, say,

Neil Young or Francis Rossi,
instead, I looked more like an unkempt member of the
Jackson Five

Big Hair was a sign of decadence,
a lowering of standards
a defiance of authority,
of all that was good, upright and holy,
the start of a slipperyslope into
debauchery, drug-fueled orgies
anarchy:
The end of civilization as we know it.

My observation that Ludwig Van Beethoven
didn't support a short back and sides
was not well received ⁄⁄

Old man and son

He wanted a son who would
listen to opera,
discuss Dickens politely,
vote Liberal,
wear a tie on Sundays,
and keep his hair respectably short.

Instead,
he got a rugby playing, left-wing
beer drinker, into Prog Rock and Folk Music.

I must be a disappointment.

No Words

I was three pints down when I heard,
it had been a good night, up till then.
But, mother + mobile = important.
Very important.

It was not the first time I'd grieved
for a young brave gone too soon,
a bud that would never bloom,
but it was the first
as an adult,
    as a man.

The first time they had looked to me.

What were they looking for?
Words of hope? Comfort? Encouragement?
There were no words.

Why? they said, Why?
I had no answer.

Sure, I could have made something up,
rehearsed some eloquent lines,
but there is no comfort in lies
however well meant.

Instead, I gave my naked soul,
open wound of my grief,
broken strength of my love.
We clung,
drowning,
salt-water cheeks stinging:
mingled tears and unspoken words

Thus, they knew,
They knew all I couldn't say ⁄⁄

Remembering Uncle Ray

I'm sad but in a gentle way,
eyes may moisten, but they won't cry,
not today.
It's a sadness that smiles in a far-off way
A wistful, distant, dreamy way that lingers on the lips
A sad that slides through the years
and smiles at memories
Memories lit by Christmases and weddings
It's a sad that floats around my edges,
but can't get hold
A sad that won't destroy or tear the soul
A sad that can't defile the past,
but one that keeps the past alive
Yes, I am sad today,
but in an easy, gentle way ⁄⁄

Bumping into Baz

"You remember Baz; played scrum-half."
Well, I *do* remember Baz,
but I don't recognise this greying chap
wheezing from his climb up from the basement loos.
"Richard," I say to his beer-blank face –
"played centre."
A light in the fog tells me
he knows the name if not the face.
We fumble through small talk,
the usual "How do you do's,"
and "What you up to's"
I learn Baz is up to "The Same Old Thing"
What "The Same Old Thing" is, I can't grasp.
Baz learns I live overlooking the sea in Newquay
Where I keep two llamas
and repair Morris Minors;
Well, he'll never remember, let alone check.
"Another pint, Baz?"
His glass is downed and slaps the bar in one swift movement.
That's the thing with Baz –
he never could pass:
a serious flaw in a scrum-half.

Hottest Summer since '76

Beneath the grey sky,
a well-passed-their-best underwear-grey sky,
a tumble-dryer-rolling, left-out-to-be-forgotten sky;
I walk along weed-cracked concrete paths,
Heel-hardened soil paths,
sodden, grass-skirted, nettle-guarded paths
still ankle-busting fissured from the heatwave.
What a heatwave!
The hottest summer since '76,
for those who can remember '76,
when brazen, uninhibited hippies
set up camp on the upland moss,
scrub-heather and whimberry commons of Mid Wales.
Locals tut-tutted,
but it didn't stop them driving up the valley
to gaze, aghast at bohemian nudity.
Mr. Deeply Offended and Miss Utterly Shocked
wrote in bold italics to local
nothing-ever-happens-here newspapers
decrying the outrageous 'Disturbance of the Peace'
(three miles from the nearest house)
and citing (with photos)
'Indecent Exposure' –
Presumably, to a passing stonechat,
or those sparsely scattered grazing sheep
 that could be bothered to lift their heads.

Eventually two bus-loads of high-helmeted policemen
dispersed the hairy, vegetarian, yoga-loving peace seekers
with their "Ynni Newclear? Dim Diolch"* stickers
to wander off and Give Peace a Chance somewhere else.

As I walk on, the sun sneaks out, briefly,
kissing the tree tops
flirting with the distant barley,

trying to regain lost ground.
With my heart back in '76,
I watch the sun disappear,
and smile.

*"Nuclear Power? No Thanks" ⁄⁄

Train ride to Paddington

Whenever I travel to Paddington,
he joins me.
I don't go often, but,
when I do, he always joins me.

Silent, we slip back through time's thick fog,
revisit our ten-year-old selves,
wild hair, big grins, leaning over the rail
in a bonfire night press photo;
there's a third boy with us,
but he's lost in the fog.

We race through the park,
past the 'Cyclists Dismount' sign
chasing the tom boy on her chopper,
ginger hair a beacon in the fog,
fog which stole her face, stole her name

We're at the carnival laughing,
pea shooters popping at the floats;
fighting his elder brother;
we're shooting bicycle pumps like water pistols
over the neighbour's fence;
we're listening to Aladdin Sane, he shows me the lyrics,
we're laughing again at the naughty word;
we're in trouble.
Whenever the fog lifts, we're in trouble.
We're in trouble for getting into trouble.

The train hurries on.
Long ago our paths split,
our troubles followed us,
somewhere along the line
he made an unscheduled exit,
left his troubles on the train

(mine still haunt me)
He never would make Paddington
He never would make twenty-six

I continue my journey wrapped in fog

Whenever I travel to Paddington,
he joins me,
he always joins me.
But I arrive alone,
    always alone. ⁄⁄

Hometown Visit

Reasons for visits are decreasing one by one,
but still, I return, seek recognition in strangers' faces;
painting colour into grey, sketching hair onto bald tops,
realigning contours of pot bellies,
airbrushing out walking sticks and wrinkles.
Each year, imagination stretched further
Each year, my chance of success smaller
and the desire to succeed,
 smaller still ⁄⁄

Sixpence

A shy, skinny girl she was;
in a skinny floral dress
and an ill-knit pastel cardy.
Lived with her mum in the next village,
if either could be called a village.
True, ours had a chapel-
no pub or shop, but a chapel -
not Baptist or Presbyterian mind,
no, some other sort.
With true Protestant tribal allegiance
we shunned the
chapel of dubious theology;
best drive five miles to be on the safe side,
so to speak,
than walk 200 yards and risk heresy.

The shy, skinny girl's village
lay across the valley;
a shamble of whitewash and slate grey,
as if the god of rural affairs
got bored and hurled a
handful of cottages to pepper the far hillside.

I went there once,
post eleven-plus summer holidays
Climbing up the zig-zagging unmade track
to the ramshackle home of
the shy, skinny girl.
Today you'd call it a
'character' cottage
with 'original' features.
Back then it was plain old-fashioned;
no way to afford central heating.

They were poor,
not modern poor
eating takeaways, full-Sky-subscription poor,
but single-mum-working-all-day-to-get-by-poor.

As I left
her mum gave me sixpence

I also left with a strange stirring,
a pre-teen awakening.
The sun was slowly dawning,
reddening my cheeks with embarrassment.
But, it was a late winter, Arctic sun;
barely made it above the horizon.

September brought a new school,
a different school bus;
life moved on.
Sixpence became two and a half new pence.
As for the shy, skinny girl,
well,
she was forgotten;
almost... ⁄⁄

Those Eyes

Her smoking eyes meet mine across the table,
tinting my cheeks, wrapping my body and stifling my voice:
my words stillborn.
My eyes seek refuge in the far corners of the room,
or on my plate of never shrinking food which I force down
my ever-shrinking throat
 – like piped icing through a clenched fist.

Yet I, the rabbit before the stoat, have to glance at those
torturing eyes;
twist the rack to which I'm chained.

At last, the final forkful challenges me from the plate,
I rehearse my lines in what remains of my jellied brain.
"I'm going to the park to play football with my mates."
No, too long, too long.
"I'm off to play footie" – guess I could manage that.
"I'm off to play footie," no deeper, must sound deeper:
"I'm off to play footie".

I squeeze in the last mouthful mercilessly
Mum beats me to it: "Why don't you take Veronic for a walk."
My hesitation fatal – I glance at those eyes,
smoke replaced by fire.
"OK," squeaks my inner rabbit.

Luckily, Veronic is no talker, my French limited to "J'ai
Faim"
 – inappropriate as I feel like a stuffed turkey –
or "Ou e la Gare"?
What! How would she know where the "Gare" is?

Entering the woods, the path narrows,
but not narrow enough! We walk side by side,

my left arm flapping strangely, as if it had never been on a walk before,
brushes her hip, knocks her elbow, touches her hand.
Her hand!
She grabs my hand!
My arm looses any last remaining semblance of rhythm,
swings too fast, too slow, it's too long, too short....
And the clasp – do I squeeze – how hard?
I don't want to crush this hand, that lily, so delicate, so soft;
I had only ever grabbed blokes before – playing rugby of course
you know – manly stuff – this is a different species, so fragile, so tender, so smooth.
I relax my grip – oh no! what if she thinks I'm a wimp;
I squeeze tighter – too tight!

The stile saves me, she swings a leg over, her short skirt riding a bit too high
– I mean to look away, but ...
She lands, gazelle-graceful
She turns,
those eyes,
they draw me in,
helpless,
her lips meet mine
I grip the stile
The malaise gripping my throat and arms spreads to my legs;
in fact, only a very little part of me seems to be working.

And that is how our holiday romance began.
We promised to write, but,
I was no writer,
and evidently,
neither was she. ◢

I never expected ...

I never expected when we first kissed,
pressed up against the youth club wall;
or sitting in a field, sheep idly watching,
you in your new denim jacket
(the most expensive thing you had ever bought);
or standing in the glow of the street lamp
eating newspaper-wrapped fish 'n' chips,
I never expected our lives together
would travel beyond Hereford or Aberystwyth,
never expected all these years later
you'd still be blonde, still be beautiful,
we'd still be sharing newspaper-wrapped fish 'n' chips. ⁄⁄

Firework

I'm just a firework
Alone in the dark
I'll always be nothing
Without your spark.

I'm just a sparkler
You are the light
Together our love
Will sparkle tonight.

L.O.V.E.

Before we met, love was a four-letter word
'I love you,' a three-word phrase
We were two lonesome hearts
Now we are one ⁄⁄

Following Too Much Cheese

Last night I dreamt you were here with me:
it's a hard memory to take,

knowing,
when I awake,
you'll be gone;

I let sleep cradle us as long as possible. ⁄⁄

Fingerprints On My Mind

She left fingerprints on my mind
Quite by chance one afternoon.
I never really asked her to, or why,
But she strode in wearing jackboots
And slung her coat across the nearest hook
Where it hung like the shed skin of some reptile –
A reptile who was hunting anything that moved –
And so it was that she swallowed me whole
After crushing the life from my mortal body
Only to find I didn't care much for my body anyway
Then turning to my mind,
Found it impossible to control –
But, like a finch in a cage,
It couldn't escape either.
Consequently, she caught it
Just long enough
To make an impression. ⁄⁄

Jessica

Jessica moved like moonlight dancing across the lake
She could flit like the sun through the trees
She could soothe your soul like soft summer rain
And would glide through a crowd like the breeze

She could trust like a child,
Stand like a queen
Tend to your wounds like a nurse
Could hear you call, step into your dreams
Trespass your mind like a curse

Smile like an angel,
Laugh like an imp
Her face a destroyer of Troy
Sinking a thousand ships with her lips
Leaving you wrecked between heartbreak and joy

She gave me those lips, gave me a song
gave me the smooth warmth of her thighs
I sailed the pure white touch of her skin
And was lost in the blue of her eyes

But passion and lust strangled our thoughts
Senses fell before youthful desire
Love and wisdom don't go hand in hand
When your heart is fighting the fire

We hid from the truth, but truth doesn't change
It only gets buried by lies
The debris of pain that we left behind
Was all we could see with blind eyes

Years rolled by till we met quite by chance
At a do for a mutual friend

In those three minutes it took us to dance
We discovered some things never end

Jessica moved, a cloud over a lake,
A shadow that drifts through the trees
Moving through summer after that spring
She melted away
On the breeze ⁄⁄

I missed you today

I missed you today,
alone in the woods
except for Dog
and 50 strangers all "Good Morning"ing
all giving each other that look to say
'Put that dog on a lead,' or
'Let that dog run free'.
I'm in the dog-run-free team,
but then, I didn't take out a loan
for a pampered pedigree,
who might be tainted by a mongrel's sniff

I missed you,
amongst the beauty of the bare birch,
bronzed bracken and semi-frost;
the puddles too took up teams – frozen, or thawed –
but most gave up and lingered somewhere in between.
I saw four deer,
staring at me through trunks and brambles, before turning,
their white behinds bob-bobbing into the unknown –
I missed you more then:
a moment we could have shared
and added to our memories.

I knew the day we met

I knew the day we met
Before words were spoken
Before friendships germinated,
budded and blossomed
Before lives intertwined,
interlaced

But knowledge doesn't deaden pain
Doesn't lighten up the midnight sky
Doesn't stave off the winter's cold
or soften sorrow's rain

That's why I'm in the kitchen,
half-dressed, drink in hand,
cooking omelettes
dancing to Madonna,
tears in my eyes,
unsure if I'm trying to remember;
or trying to forget ⁄⁄

When the dogs have left

When the dogs have left,
their slippered walkers settled down,
around the village, sea-black green,
doors are bolted for the night
leaving random squares of golden light

Rooks to the rookery clatter,
and silence settles like a cloak
on crow and scarecrow alike,
the twitter of birds fades and dies
and bats emerge to rule the skies

Pipistrelle above the garden dart
or Daubentons above still blackness
twist and turn for moth or gnat,
hare and deer feast freely on the crops -
a ghosted owl into the shadow drops

Newt and toad move moistly through the moss
slugs up stalks of lupins slide
to sate their foliole appetite
hedgehogs patrol herbaceous borders
explore the patio's hidden corners

Badgers snuffle from their set – and yet
we, in forts of brick and curtained glass
let TV rule day's dying hours
and climbing up our wooden hill
we fumble for the bedroom light
and miss the waking of the night

Village Fox

From beneath the garden shed
or, materializing from the scrub of No Man's Land,
he appears
rust-red among the darkening greens and browns,
eyes probing every shadowed corner,
seeking out shifting grey on grey.
Nose tracing the contours of scent,
mapping the invisible highways of a world we can never enter.
Ears twitching in the frost light, scanning the silence.

Noiseless as moonrise,
subtle as leaf-fall,
he glides through the privet hedge,
down the moss-clad, starlit lane,
past wood-smoke scented, curtained cottages,
name-plated garden gates, bare-boughed apple orchards,
until suddenly:
pad, pad, clip clip,
silent as smoke, he blends into the shadows.
The couple pass by hand in hand,
confident in their belief –
there are no foxes in their village.

The Passing of 1000 Gulls

As the sun ignites the western shore,
starts the slide of day
into the haze of tomorrow's memories,
from the North, in waves, they come,
curling, swirling,
silhouettes against the softly greying, high- clouded sky.
The dreams of a thousand sleeps, poured from a kaleidoscope,
turning, unfurling.
Individuals swoop, dive and double-back
but the flock migrates inexorably southwards,
shrinking to specks;
under-bellies catching the dying rays;
like glitter, they flutter and fall,
vanish beyond the distant trees,
settling in the silent plateau of my mind. ⁄⁄

I Picked up the Present
Not long after Christmas 2021

I picked up the present
I picked for you,
rolled it in my palm as I rolled you through
my mind across the frosted lawn,
beneath the bare- branched trees,
trees that you so loved;
the leafless ash, the fruitless plum,
holly stripped of its jewels, now that the fieldfares have come;
pine, trunk glowing copper in the evening sun,
the overgrown lilac no one sees, its slender limbs
twisting, reaching, lost amongst tangles of branch and leaf

And which tree are you?
The ash? – too dull
Plum? – too sweet
Holly? – too fierce
Pine? – too proud
The lilac?
The beautiful lilac
The anarchic, enigmatic,
wild-scented lilac;
out of place,
mocked by slaves to convention.
Too free to conform to the norm
(as if "normal" was a thing to be cherished),
taking the line of least expectation -
overshadowed -
the overgrown lilac no one sees,
– until it blossoms.
And then:
You fling out colour among the greens
Throw light into life's shadows
Wear a rainbow in society's rain
Dance to a tune you alone can hear
Stand in the tempest while others bend in the breeze

I roll in my palm the present
I picked for you
and wish you here among the trees ⧸⧸

The Silence of Yesterday

The silence of yesterday still echoes,
fading like scent that lingers
amongst curtain folds and closed up rooms

Opening a pane, today's noises rush in,
with a mix of fading blossom and rain,
diluting perception.

Late summer dusk settles,
silence swells, filling empty spaces,
the outside world lays defeated,
a lone owl cries;
bruising memories emphasising loneliness.

Last time we met

      The daffs were out,
gently swaying to the rhythm of the day;
above two buzzards slow-waltzed before the sun,
which thrust itself unbidden into your overwarm front room,
and I ate your last two hobnobs

The last time we met, we talked:
We talked about your
100-year-old violin,
The goats down on the farm,
The cruise ship job that never was,
Your record collection.
I snaffled *Eine Kleine Nachtmusik* and *Fingal's Cave,*
I told you I'd bought a 1959 Buddy Holly album for a fiver in Whitchurch,
You asked who Buddy Holly was –
I changed the subject – told you I wrote poetry:
I didn't read you any;
You didn't ask.

In all our years
We never spoke with voices of the heart
Or talked of love
Or dreams.
Emotion's fluff never shook the steady lips of men
who'd learnt from other men that's how men should be.

Last time we met
No one knew it would be the last time,
The last time we'd share cups of tea,
Pore over old maps,
Exchange news face to face;
Our last chance
to share a hug

A tender word
A tear of loss, joy, sorrow, regret

The last time we met,
We shook our formal goodbyes,
Parting to live alone the distant lives,
We'd lived out all our lives;

And shed our tears in solitude ⁄⁄

The Real You

My friend
somewhere between the coffee shop-latte-laughter
and the tear-soaked pillow,
between the air-brushed perfection you show the world
and the razor trembling in your hand
as your naked body lies to your mirror
stands the real You.

Somewhere, running from the You your parents tried to build,
hiding from the You moulded by High Street fashion dummies,
inside the You stuffed into a chocolate box,
bound in ribbons, labelled, packaged, over-priced,
beneath the You you've tried to create
from scraps of others' inexperience,
second-hand aspirations, and hand-me-down expectations:
somewhere beneath all this tinsel and dust stands the real You,
the beautiful You, the unique and lovely You,
the You loved just for being You.

I passed a group of moist-eyed men

Warning! This poem is a reflection on the aftermath of a suicide which might be upsetting

I passed a broken body,
sheeted in the street
I passed a group of moist-eyed men,
grief dripping from their cheeks

I passed pinch-faced young ladies,
with eyes that dare not see
I passed the waiting curious,
necks craned to take a peek
while young high-viz vested police stood guard,
trying not to think

I passed a waiting ambulance, too late it got the call
Lights, like some bad habit hard to break, bouncing blue
off the shelter wall

I passed the council workmen, orange collars turned up
against the rain
Who scrubbed the man's last marks from earth, and sluiced
them down the drain

That night I slept with moist-eyed men and young yellow-
vested guards
When I awoke, I called a friend just to ask them
how they are

A Crack Appeared

A crack appeared years ago,
      it let the darkness in.
A crack appeared in my youth
      it let the darkness in.

Sometimes, it closes up,
but never really heals:
      just keeps the darkness in.

A crack appeared,
like an old ship
tossed upon the seas
the wooden slats open up
and let the waters in,
so, each downward trough
lets more darkness in.

A crack appeared years ago,
      and let the darkness in //

The Valley of the Shadow

Sometimes
the Valley of the Shadow
is so deep
so dark
there is no light

but
worst of all
I don't even want the light

Sorry for being so rubbish

Sorry for being so rubbish today
Sorry for being such a useless friend
for not 'being there' for you
for not taking you by the hand to walk amongst the blue bells,
for not picking the rose,
for not serenading from below the balcony.
Sorry for not singing, not dancing,
not coming out of my shell, but
that's how I feel today.
Like a mollusc,
locked inside myself, the door clamped shut. ⁄⁄

To A Friend

I know what it is to be human,
I too, have felt the crack of wood on bone,
felt the shredded skin of knee on roughened tarmac,
or the deeper sting of shame,
my faults paraded across the stage.

I too have known the loss of friends departed,
some though choice; seeking a better life,
Others? Well, fate ordained their unsought departure.
I too have known the stabbing wound of betrayal,
its premeditation piercing deeper than any loss.

I too have known the dark road of despair,
blindly groping deeper into the unknown,
self shrinking to worthlessness,
its charred remains buried deep
within the ashes of yesterday's dreams.

True, I don't know what it's like to be You,
but I know what it is to be human,
to seek the shoulder,
to crave the hug,
to search storm-blackened skies for the rainbow.

I too know how to lend the shoulder,
give the hug,
reach out into the abyss,
hold the hand in the storm,
lend the raincoat

I know what it is to rise,
to feel the mending of bone,
the sealing of the scar
to shake off the ashes
and return to the light.

Lean on me.
I know what is it to be human.

The Visit

His wife wasn't in when I called;
the debris of neglect spoke louder than his voice

How long had she been away?
Too long by the look of it:
every, mug, plate, bowl, jug,
knife, fork, spoon, pot, pan and pig trough
pressed into service.
His tea table stacked high
with less space than a Soweto slum.
I picked my way over discarded wellies;
kindling (on its way in)
an ash pan (on its way out),
a spade, a billhook, the dog – too idle to move.
He gestured to the least cluttered chair;
I sat on hessian sacks
and an unwaxed waxed jacket,
twine hanging from its ripped pockets –
accepted the cup of tea – black –
hoping the boiling of the water would suffice.
I asked after his daughters, all grown up now of course.
I didn't ask about his wife;
the wall calendar – a golden leafed view:
Swallow Falls, October 2016,
told me all I needed to know ▰

Haikus

The follies of youth
too distant to remember
too close to forget ⁄⁄

Winds of change blowing
fanning the flames of man's fire,
silent dust settles ⁄⁄

Crisis, what crisis?
Life is as it ever was:
heads still stuck in sand ⁄⁄

What is Truth?

What is Truth – and will that Truth remain?

Is my truth your truth?
Is truth a shade of grey
or
black & white,
right or wrong?

Does Truth change with time and space?
Will your truth change with age?

Is your truth worth fighting for?
Is mine worth dying for?

Are the truths of today the lies of tomorrow?

What colour is the shadow on a whitewashed wall?

An Old Man Told Me

      How he longed to return
                              home

We all called him Stan,
No one could get their English-speaking tongues
around all those Z's and clashing consonants

He left a young man,
Herded by SS badged uniforms
shouting a language he couldn't understand
vividly translated by Jack Boots and rifle butts

Through a finger-high panorama
squeezed between the slats
he watched his childhood dreams slip away,
slip away with the passing park,
the forbidding – yet enticing – wood,
the minnow rich stream.
He watched youth's lusts and hunger vanish with the
dancehall and street cafés.
He watched his ambitions, hopes and plans disappear as
the town shrank from view until,
only the steeple, a pin prick on the horizon, blinked the last
flicker of evening light

Through countless hours he watched passing farms, towns,
forests, rivers,
hills, seas of sunflowers,
He watched stone faced border guards
He watched strange towns with familiar names
Wien, Linz, Salzburg

He told me all this and more
He told me of the Farm, the valley and the hills
He told me of the Swastika, starvation and slavery

And he told me of the night-time flight,
days of desperation passed in undergrowth, abandoned barns
terror filled nightly navigation of the Alpine passes,
heading west, picking bilberry's:
the Border –
a final Now or Never, All or Nothing,
Do or Die gasp for freedom.

He told me all this over milky tea one afternoon,
by now Hammer and Sickle had replaced Swastika,
Fences and landmines cut a scar dividing
his homeland from his home,
but despite this,
despite cream scones, battered cod, cricket,
Morcombe and Wise, the BBC,
warm beer and Yorkshire Pudding,
Stan still longed to go home.

Seeking Open Water

trapped in a Norwegian fjord
desperately seeking open water.
beneath the pounding of the guns,
amongst the splintering of the deck,
they worked and fought,
beneath the pounding of the guns,
the screaming of the men,
the rocking of the boat,
the able seamen worked and fought,
beneath the pounding of the guns,
the screaming of the men,
the stillness of the dead,
the screaming of the Stukas,
the crashing of the deck,
the pounding of the guns,
the screaming of the Stukas,
the screaming of the Stukas,
the screaming of the Stukas,
night after night after night after night
after D Day,
after VE Day,
after demob,
after dark,
after night after night,
the screaming of the Stukas....
after night after night
seeking open water
night after night ⁄⁄

Dancing beneath the Doodlebugs

Are we wandering down the garden path
gazing up at the doodlebugs,
lounging in those gardens
the gardens of our papier mâché houses
all neatly arranged
on ancient flood plains

Are we building our steeples and minarets
of china and clay
on the cliff edge
chanting
"We are safe,"
"We are safe"?

Are we sailing yachts
of balsa and brass
into the hurricane,
singing, "It's only a breeze,"
"It's only a breeze,"
"We'll ride the storm like our fathers before
and when we return, we'll build tree-houses
for Ellie and Zack
deep in the forest,
where they can build fires
from desert-dry sticks
and toast marshmallows in safety".

Are we riding into the eye of the storm
when we could escape through the eye of the needle,
if only we were prepared to pay the price,
or would we rather sacrifice

our glaciers
polar bears
island nations

Rotterdam
Amsterdam
New York
London
our forests

Forsaking Proven Science for Gung-Ho foolery

Are we wandering down the garden path
in paper hats,
singing songs,
throwing confetti
while dancing beneath the doodlebugs? ⁄⁄

In 1944, during WWII, flying bombs – known as doodlebugs – were launched at London; my Granddad was deaf and hadn't heard about these new weapons, so when one flew overhead, he wandered down the garden path gazing up in fascination.

Colours of our Land

There are no blue birds over
these white cliffs of Dover
just grey clouds
thick with sorrow and shame
and a handful of scavenging crows
perched on thatched ridges
of black timbered houses
gazing down with murderous,
coal-diamond eyes
on the quaint village green
scanning for hapless prey
amongst cucumber Pimm's
and eccentric whims
of the Old School Tie Way,
bought with the Empire's gold
built with the sweat of her slaves,
where pink rose-rambled arches
and St. George's Day marches
meet under the red cross of the saint,
the Christian sign of salvation,
which flutters from cricket pavilions
and towers of churches,
this emblem – once raised in glory
hangs, a limp flag of betrayal
as we turn our backs
on our former lands
and debate the bodies
washed up on the sands,
while washing their scarlet
blood from our hands.

Gravestones

It came to this:
A handful of lines
Etched in stone:
A name
A date,
Loved
And missed by other names
Etched
Into newer stones.

Where they drowned the Witches

"...and this," she said, "is where they
drowned the witches ...."

I stared into the clear, dark depths:
the rounded stones
smooth as skulls,
long rippling waterweed
reaching for the light:
shreds of a tattered gown
held forever in the depths,
the fallen branch:
bleached twig-fingers
gnarled, grasping.

Along the bank we stood
enthralled
joined by a gaping crowd
locked in superstitions,
chained by fear,
trembling before the black-clad priest,
his voice booming out damnation,
praying for the soul,
killing the body.

Our guide's voice droned on
"...the nearby monastery....
...the cotton industry...
...diversity of wildlife..."
none of this I took in,
but I can show you,
exactly
where they drowned the witches. //

Just Walking Home
aka It's different for girls

I was just walking home
alone
content
confident
feeling the cool air,
sucking in the night
stepping to the sounds of the forgotten day;
 a bat flickered
 a moth celebrated a streetlamp halo

I was just walking home
I saw no shifting in the shadows
heard no breath on the breeze
took no long way round to seek comfort from streetlights
no keys bunched in clenched fingers
no echo of footsteps tracing mine,
step for step,
turn for turn,
closer,
closer

I was just walking home
my front door
blue in this half-dark,
path shadowed by the hedge
the latch turns
lamplight welcomes.
Inside
I pick some music
pour a dram
close my eyes
and remember
she was
just walking home ⁄⁄

The Kiss

A moment passing,
lips on lips,
the dog lazy,
slack on the lead
in a carefree current
of dread-locks and crew cuts,
patched jackets, designer tops,
scuffed high-laced boots,
painted toes in faded sandals.
The sun inches its timeless arc
casting a shadow:
ladies joined
on the weather-worn wall,
its stonework as heedless
as the passing High Street ⁄⁄

LGB with the T

It's important that T
That maligned T
That misunderstood and mistrusted T
That less than 1% T
That marginalised, despised,
confused, abused,
battered and bruised T
Alone in the dark,
stabbed in the park T
That T for teachers, tailors, truckers, traders,
taxi drivers, tax inspectors, tellers and testers

T represents Texans, Tuscans, Turks and Tatars
There's T from Tyneside, Teesside, Twickenham, Tiverton,
Tehran, Turin, Tokyo and Tupelo

T for the terrorised, traumatised, targeted, tortured

For those
Whose greatest crime is being different,
going against the flow,
standing out, standing up, being themselves.
Being who they are
being honest

It's important, that T
It represents people
Real people,
like you, like me
People who love
and are loved
People with hopes
with schemes and dreams
People with feelings
People who bleed

who fear
who shed a tear

It's important that T
Just like the L,
and the G and the B:
like you and me ⁄⁄

White Knight

The White Knight, stock-still adjacent the
crenulated white-walled castle.
He surveys the rank and file
lined up – pawns in the game,
ready to fulfill their duty,
ready to be sacrificed in the Master's gambit.

Battle commences,
at first, a slow, strategic affair,
the Knight bemoans his lot – fighting to defend the King.
"Hmmph! Some King, *so important, so crucial,* and yet –
so ineffectual, so slow.
The Queen? Now that's another story altogether,
dynamic, powerful,
(we know who wears the breeches in that household)
The King should keep her in check – dashing off hither and
thither.
And, as for that Bishop – prancing up and down after her,
vow of celibacy. Huh! I bet that cassock's seen more action
than my lance.
And he gets to wear his mitre,
Look at me, Just Look at me, the front half of a pantomime
horse,
I'm not even allowed to charge in a straight line.
Knight!? I should be called a hobbled mare.

Oh, look out! Action, here we go:
Two steps forward, one to the left, seems pretty safe,
although, must keep an eye on those pawns,
sneaky little critters, like snails, never move,
but turn your head for two minutes and who knows where
they'll be.

Oh! I'm off again, two steps right, one forward,
at least the Bishop has me covered,

the pompous 'Holier than thou' (well he is holier than me).
Wait! Where are you going, you wine-bibbing, whore-chasing,
incense-wafting, gout-riddled son of a hog-washer,
chasing after that Queen of Tarts again, leaving me exposed.
Wooah, I'm taken!

Damn, I *hate* chess!"

The Fisherman's Cottage

What memories lie hidden within these walls,
buried behind plaster, beneath floor-boards
or lost in unreached corners of the loft.

How many lives conceived,
how many births – of people long gone.
How many deaths.
Do their ghosts still haunt these rooms:
carry out their daily chores,
climb stairs through mid-air,
open a once-upon-a-time front door
to wave at neighbours passing by
on horseback down the rutted lane.

Does the fisherman still haul his eels from the Derwent,
gut them in our front room,
discarding heads on the earth-packed floor
which his cat prizes,
but ours ignore.

Hints to their memories remain:
fragments of pottery,
hooks, rusted into ceiling beams,
unexplained patterns in brickwork.
And what will we leave,
what clues for future generations.
Will our ghosts linger,
will we sit in our favourite chairs
in some futuristic lounge or high-tech kitchen,
staring at a space where once the TV stood;
will we pluck a bottle of red from the shelf,
raising a toast to the good old days.

Walking the Days Away

Walking the days away
Pounding memories into oblivion
Dodging Life's cajoling whisper,
Echoing in my empty glass

Hugging the blankness of my thoughts
Wrapping loneliness around my senses
Blending the soothing voice of solitude into the silences
Left between the heartbeats
Drumming their lifeline in my ear

Your beauty etched inside my lids forever

Girl with the Violin

She entered,
barely noticed amongst the
toing and froing, froing and toing,
passed through the room, silent and cool
as the breeze that chased her through the open doorway;
a few half-glances slid her way
before returning to the present,
to partners, lovers, friends, fellow strangers,
to their real ale or pinot grigio.
Conversations rose like sparrows,
stories spread their wings,
theories and counter-theories ascended like doves,
and through the chattering hum
she took her place:
the girl with the violin.

She stroked the strings,
gentle as an angel's kiss,
tender as a lover's smile, soft as April dew.
Music flowed like milk and honey,
wrapped the room in a velvet hug;
the tune rose like a butterfly,
hovered on the stillness before descending
as cherry blossom drifts slowly from the bough.
The twittering sparrows fell silent,
the doves dropped meekly to roost,
purity filled the air, filled the soul,
eclipsing the here and now.

And every eye was turned, every lip was tight,
every tongue was still, every ear was open,
all were quiet, lost in the moment,
haunted by the melody,
swallowed by the ghost of beauty,
enchanted by the spell; and in that spell found peace,
every spirit was cleansed, every heart knew love – if only briefly.

And for that while, everything surrendered, surrendered to the girl with the violin. ✒

Take These Words

Take These Words
Take them,
Take them to your darkened room
Hide them with your secrets
They will share your truth

Take these lips
Bury them in your purse
In the silence of your night
They will answer your fear

Take these hands
Hold them
Fold them in your loneliness
They will share your solitude

Take these words
These lips
These hands
Show them your soul
Share them with your heart
They will share your life

Acknowledgements

Thanks to Rose, Alan and Fiona and all at York Spoken Word for their support, encouragement and inspiration

Other anthologies and collections available from Stairwell Books

An Anxiety of Poets in their Natural Habitat	Amina Alyal
First of All I Wrote Your Name	Winston Plowes
Sleeve Heart	Eleanor May Blackburn
Goldfish	Jonathan Aylett
Strike	Sarah Wimbush
Marginalia	Doreen Hinchliffe
The Estuary and the Sea	Jennifer Keevill
In	Between	Angela Arnold
Quiet Flows the Hull	Clint Wastling
Lunch on a Green Ledge	Stella Davis
there is an england	Harry Gallagher
Iconic Tattoo	Richard Harries
Herdsmenization	Ngozi Olivia Osuoha
On the Other Side of the Beach, Light	Daniel Skyle
Words from a Distance	Ed. Amina Alyal, Judi Sissons
Fractured	Shannon O'Neill
Unknown	Anna Rose James, Elizabeth Chadwick Pywell
When We Wake We Think We're Whalers from Eden	Bob Beagrie
Awakening	Richard Harries
Starspin	Graehame Barrasford Young
A Stray Dog, Following	Greg Quiery
Blue Saxophone	Rosemary Palmeira
Steel Tipped Snowflakes 1	Izzy Rhiannon Jones, Becca Miles, Laura Voivodeship
Where the Hares Are	John Gilham
The Glass King	Gary Allen
Gooseberries	Val Horner
Poetry for the Newly Single 40 Something	Maria Stephenson
Northern Lights	Harry Gallagher
More Exhibitionism	Ed. Glen Taylor
Lodestone	Hannah Stone
Learning to Breathe	John Gilham
Throwing Mother in the Skip	William Thirsk-Gaskill
New Crops from Old Fields	Ed. Oz Hardwick
The Ordinariness of Parrots	Amina Alyal

For further information please contact rose@stairwellbooks.com

www.stairwellbooks.co.uk
@stairwellbooks

www.ingramcontent.com/pod-product-compliance
Lightning Source LLC
Chambersburg PA
CBHW031212090426
42736CB00009B/881